Musings

A Collection of Reflective Poems

Avril Dias

BookLeaf Publishing

India | USA | UK

Dedication

To my mother;
to whom I always read my thoughts to first and
who is always the first to read my thoughts.

Preface

"Musings: A Collection of Reflective Poems" is a culmination of the things that often go unnoticed and that often feels indescribable. This collection was borne out of my immense love for painting with words and writing on paper what I see when I close my eyes. As you venture into familiar territories, I hope these poems can add something special to the experiences you may have already experienced. This collection is a melting pot of emotions, feelings, colours, tastes, smells, and sights; that I would like for you to experience as if it were the first time again.

Acknowledgements

When I planted the seed for this book, you helped me watch over it, as the seedling sprouted into a tree. To my mother; for your keen eye and honest feedback; who was always there at the other end of the line. Your thoughtful critiques helped me see things from more angles that I could sometimes see.

1. The Beginning

An orange glow;
the light of the outside world,
diffusing softly through the curtains of my mother's
womb.
I imagine an orange sky and a flash of light as the air
rushed through my lungs.
A cry of joy and a cry so shrill,
the rhythm, matching the pace of my heartbeat.
A siren to signal I was here,
and the feeling of my mother's skin,
to know I was truly safe.
I imagine a layer of fog,
veiling my eyes,
I age and it slowly lifts,
I can then see the world more clearly each day.
The colours jumping at my face,
the air tickling my nose and I whine;
but my parents worry I may be hungry.
I see two familiar faces,
two voices that are engraved in my brain.
I can now recognise them; they are my people; now and
forever.
The days pass, but I know nothing of time;

for the knowledge of time is yet to come,
I am yet to understand how the world turns.

2. Growing Pains

A striking pain ran up my thighs, for days, on and off.
My bones tightened as they prepared to grow.
At times it hurt to walk; times that I did not understand.
The paediatrician demanded: walk on, through the pain,
the first possible instance of being thrust into the
unknown and being told to sail.
The pain vanished, as the paediatrician had promised.
Cautious as I was with the pain in my thighs,
I now knew it could have been only in my mind.
The mind can be an abyss, a maze to enter; a lifetime of
constant navigation.
The years painted and re-painted me,
as I became an ever-evolving version of myself.
Stumbling on rocks planted before I could expect it;
learning to regain my balance and learning to foresee the
stones before they appeared.
Every placement of the rock I memorized;
every time I learned to walk again.
And so, bruises from tripping dotted my body.
I realize I cannot stop the bruises and the dotting,
I now just had to embrace my coat of polka dots.
I imagine, growing is a journey,
of hesitating, resisting, and dreading to wear your polka-
dotted coat.

But this coat shows the wealth you possess,
the power from your growing pains.
It is not a veil of shame,
But a vestment of honour.

3. Through a Moving Window

Sunlight on your eyes like a flickering light bulb,
the rays bolt through the running branches.
A smear of colour you see, but when you focus, the
world outside moves with you.
The outside, distorted by water's veil,
In each droplet, the world exists; a thousand times.
Some droplets win the race,
the others leisurely cruising in the wind.
I see the world through a moving window,
yet so little of the world I see.
A figure on the grass, in a house, in a tree;
each in a world of their own,
of which, only a flash I behold.
The wind, like shaking paper and whispering thunder in
my ears,
dries my eyes as I fight my lashes to keep them open.
I see excerpts already written, while each continues
penning their script.
From the morning's flashing sunlight to the night's
blinking headlights,
in the midnight blue, the moon follows,
keeping my side as I glance out the moving window.
Then I am rocked into a slumber by the dancing on the

craters,
tiny droplets of rain fall gently onto my hands,
only to wake and notice no rain, only a sleeping hand.
The rain finally arrives,
a resounding drum of the pearls from the sky,
a forced silence now.
The deafening percussion, a nudge to once again-
look outside the moving window.

4. On the stage, in the wings

The fog, interlacing every figure,
The stage, covered in a white wraith of smoke.
The cold gusts of air, brushing on glittery faces,
as the sun sets in the hall and the voices reduce to a
mere hum.
A zip, a cough, a rustle of paper-
the only sounds I hear before the crescendo of music
begins.
Natural half breaths and intentional full breaths,
As I exhale, the tassels on my vest jump to the rhythm of
my heart gently pounding.
As they go on before me, the show begins,
the applause brings the rain and thunder to our doorstep.
As the thunder subsides, the music clinks,
the podium turns red.
I wait to walk among the fog tinged red,
the lights bleed into the wings.
A glimpse of figures on red chairs,
And silver sparks flashing irregularly,
I advance to the stage, one last breath before I face the
light.
The light, now the only thing I see,
the circles and chairs, I can see no more.
Only the black abyss of the vast rows,

a silent countdown,

a little prayer,

staring at the skin of my palms glazed with tiny droplets

from each pore.

I feel the first vibration, the bass tickles my toes.

From there the mind takes over,

and I become one with the music.

5. Desire

An often unexplainable lure. A longing.
A beautifully painted landscape of deep-rooted emotion,
alive in your mind.
When you close your eyes, it is there, it exists- desire.
The body transcends space and travels the path your
mind has laid.
A burning fire, a spark, a rush down your spine, or a pit
in your stomach.
Just as there are people in the world, there is a multitude
of desire,
of longing, and of wanting.

Books open and close, and words seep into your brain.
They are imprinted in your memory, someday waiting to
be running wild on paper.
As the words dash towards the finish line,
you remember the longing for those words to win the
race.
Months spent singing the same song, with the same
words, from the same book.
Like bustling atoms in your brain, waiting for an out,
your test awaits, and your desire to do well now in
motion.

As we walk through life's flight of stairs, we lose flight,
fall, and tumble.
Rolling in the mud, smeared in dirt.
Our hands clipped together; our feet, slippery from the
mud.
We learn to stand again and walk for the first time again.
We yearn to walk the stairs of life again. A pit in your
stomach, a fuel for change.

Sparklers in your chest from seeing something you love,
a desire to be close, to feel, to be with. A sigh after
something you could not have,
a delight at the thought that you could get something
better.
A click, a synchronised spark- love. So unique, yet the
same.
Desire, shared by all, yet different.

The love you give and the love you get,
both ignite the candle of desire- to give back even more.
The desire to care more, to love more, and to be grateful.
Gratitude is thanks for what you have, a catalyst for the
desire to be a better you.

A creative often wanders, goes on long walks,
wanders more, and is always looking, observing,
and painting with unseen colours behind their eyes

before it exists for the world.
The workshop that lies behind the eyes, a creative mind,
longs for an outlet too.
A desire to create, for themselves and the world.
To bring the products of the workshop to the place that
exists before us.

Desire is everywhere.
It is sweet, subtle, fiery, raging, or somber.
It is abstract, often goes unnoticed,
but like an invisible string, it tugs at us now and then.
Desire is a longing- it is our heart beating like a drum;
the resounding reverberation summoning what is ours,
was ours or what can be ours.

6. Dreams

In one place, then the next, travelling miles in
milliseconds.
Vivid in sleep, often gone by morning.
They say it reflects your unconscious; a message
encrypted in hieroglyphs.
Hieroglyphs you can seldom decipher;
your body in bed, your mind running free.
Some imprint themselves, so that when you close your
eyes,
you can see them in the light too.
Of worlds, known and unknown.
In a sudden spiral, you see the sky twisting like a
tornado.
You feel your stomach fly as you drop down,
only for it to jolt your eyelids open,
to stop spinning at the sight of the spinning fan.
Animals murmuring like people, twirling on a dance
floor ,
completing a quest or
being an aerial spectator,
to the herds of wildebeest rushing into the blue lakes in
search of water,
while you watch in awe from the balcony of a
skyscraper.

As you fall asleep, the tape rolls, the projection now on
the dark inside of your eyelids.
A theatre, only for you, as you sleep back, relaxed.
Now enjoy the show, specially curated for you,
a time-lapse of what your eyes have seen during the day,
only now, decorated with a hundred tassels.
Maybe it is not an encrypted message or a signal for
action.
Maybe it is your body taking a break,
retiring for the day,
as it spends its free time,
every night,
watching you dream.

7. Silence

An absence of noise but a breeder of emotions.
Standing in the way of the blowing breeze,
while it runs through your hair, your eyes closed, a
silence so loud.
Staring as the sun meets the horizon, the waves
interlocking with grains of sand.
A rhythmic crescendo and ultimate dispersal of water
over the vast expanse of broken rocks.
Drops of rain, tumbling down steps of leaves, and
the rustle of blades of grass at dusk.
The quiet lullaby that puts you to sleep and
what remains lingering in the air, when remembering
those fallen into eternal sleep.
A prolonged ringing when all noise suddenly ceases to
exist,
the absence of sound pushing against your ears.
The noise, cut out by the water surrounding you as you
dive, and
the song of birds as the light breaks through the clouds
in the morning.
You hear this in silence
when you listen and not merely hear.
You hear the ticking of the clock,
the beating of your heart, and the buzz of the television,

when you filter out the noise and hear the tunes of the
world.
There is rhythm in the mundane,
there is music in the silence.

8. Calm after the storm

I have seen butterflies with torn wings, perch beside me.
Grasshoppers with one less leg, climb a wall.
Bees with asymmetric wings, try and fly.
I have read about whales repairing their tail ends that
got disfigured in propellers
and how fungi tried to undo the past in Chernobyl.
When water does not have a path to flow, it carves its
own.
When the canopies of trees become jigsaws to resist
abrasions.
As a cactus keeps itself hydrated in the blistering heat
and
the moss adds colour to the white frigid landscape.
I admire the stubbornness of the barcode tags on new
utensils and
the pettiness of the turmeric in those translucent lunch
boxes.
From the single flower that stays attached to its branch
after the wind has blown away its friends,
to the pink colour behind your ear that wants to stick
with you just a little longer after Holi.
Like a permanent marker still clinging onto your shirt
after ten washes-
the world abounds in instances of lengthening roots to

reach water and

springing back after the tide has washed over.

Resilience in the face of turmoil.

Restoring the calm after the storm.

9. Seasons

Lemon green leaves, young and steady,
next to their older counterparts.
Every day, the landscape is dotted with more colours
than the day before.
The colour rushes back to the monochromatic landscape,
as the warm breeze paints over the grasses.
The sun kisses the skin like a warm iron.
Butterflies, birds, and insects get their playground back.
Nature was dormant, now bursting with life.

The warm iron turns hot,
the air then becomes dry and the sun seems to grow
more powerful the more you perspire.
The surface of the ground, burning with transparent fire.
Stepping outside only to be stampeded by the blistering
wind that evaporates the water from the eyes,
the eyelids feel like sandpaper constantly grazing over
them.
All water, now vapour, revealing the bottoms of ponds.
Nature turns dry and the skin is glazed like freshly
watered plants.

As the skies grow heavy with the water of the earth,
the showers tip-toe in at night, easing their way to begin

performing the whole day.
As the clouds walk past each other, they feel a sudden
pinch of electricity.
Neon lights zig-zag their way across the sky,
branching out into tributaries.
The earth, distracted by the spectacle,
is shaken from its gaze by a sharp sound,
like a tower of chairs falling apart in the house above.
As the water touches the ground,
it seems as though you are crouching close to the soil to
smell the earth.
The petrichor tantalizes, with the promise of cooler days.
The colours of nature's playground, now paint the sky,
as the sun and falling pearls waltz in the heavens.

The days get shorter as the green turns to orange and
then to brown.
First, there were showers of water, now showers of dried
leaves.
The landscape gradually shrivels as the trees reveal their
bony structure.
The colour fades, once green and blue, now grey and
brown.

Fingers numb and a striking pain up your toes as the
warm water hits them for the first time.
Where breath is not invisible anymore.

The bridge of your nose being pinched by the cold and
the skin drying up like the leaves.
For the cold now will soon turn to warmth again,
the grey into green.

10. Whispers

Shhh. The movie's about to begin.
Trying to reach out over three chairs for the popcorn;
loud hushes and wandering hands.

Stomachs aching from containing laughter behind
laptops on the desks,
in a class so quiet you can hear us breathe.

The silence is most humorous in the library;
whispers turn into snorts,
while the turning pages rhythmically hiss.

Wind squeezing its way through a gap in the window, a
high-pitched whistle.
As murmurs layer over each other before a play, turning
from a hum to a hush as the lights dim.
The obvious whisper from grandma slipping a gift into
our hands,
to the calculated footsteps as the floors creek on our way
out.

The air of work turns the volume down low on those
passing by study halls
and the rushed calculations under your breath

as you stare into a blank paper waiting to be filled in.

The leaves, extend salutations of the evening to each
other
and the warm breeze prods them to start conversations.

Whispers of confession, of love, of secrets untold;
from a breathy voice to a listening ear.

Both concealing and revealing, of secrets and passionate
declarations.
Though soft and hushed,
in that moment,
a whisper weighs a whopper.

11. The world's serenade

Sweet whistles when the sun falls over the trees,
a chorus of good mornings in a hundred melodies.
Rainwater dripping from the window;
nature's metronome to which the birds sing.
The cue that plays before the announcements at the train
station and
the constant drone of the man in the stall opposite the
station as he chants 'chai!'
The galloping sound of trains on overhead tracks and
the prolonged horns blaring every peak hour.
Buzzing from the blue light of the flycatcher and
the baritone hum of the air conditioner.
The sound of reversing cars reverberating through the
parking lot and
the twinkle tune as you gaze at the numbers on the
screen in an elevator.
I sing along to the washing machine signalling a cycle is
done and
I harmonise with the microwave while I wait for the
croissant.
As the sun sets, the wind plays its instrument,
the wind chime tinkles and
the birds perform an ensemble to the wind's musical
piece.

As the day comes to an end, as the eyes close,
the serenade you never asked for- the buzz from the
wings of a mosquito;
it insists on putting on one last performance.
You plead it to leave,
with flailing hands,
eventually, it takes a bow.
The rhythmic clicks of the fan then lull you to sleep.

12. Treasure

Heaps of gold and jewels in a chest,
sparkling with iridescence and opulence.
Chains and rings and coins of heavy metal,
excavated from the earth, now worth a fortune.
What is treasure?
Gold or precious jewels or something money can buy?
Treasure is spotting a bird almost endangered,
chancing upon a four-leaf clover or
seeing the sky painted with a double rainbow.
It is also witnessing the clouds be ice-makers for the first
time in a place that rarely ever sees rain.
Meeting the right people,
befriending someone you just click with, and
having people around you who only want the best for
you.
Catching an elusive peacock run across the road,
the perfect shot through the viewfinder or
reaching a waterfall after brushing aside branches with
no end in sight.
A family heirloom,
your mother's old clothes that she now passes down to
you.
Being trusted with responsibility and
being recognised for your efforts.

Treasure is having parents who are your backbone,
who are your friends and your most honest mentors.
It is having someone other than yourself to hear the
pinball games in your head,
it is being able to share moments of challenge when it
feels a little much for your body to process.
Treasure is physical and material, but moreover,
it is an experience waiting to be experienced;
a shared sentiment and
a piece of the world that makes you smile,
even if it is just for a minute.

13. Gastronomy

Stomach growling with annoyance, echoing through the
silence,
a gnawing ache that twists within.
Your nose catches the smell of garlic tossed in butter,
the warm pungent aroma has you levitating towards its
source.
Your eyes feast on the vibrant medley of colours, the
reds, the deep greens and golden browns.
The onion creating fireworks in the pan,
the caramalised aroma tantalising your olfactory senses.
The fresh scent of basil and baking bread and
you can physically feel your mouth watering.
You bite your cheek and swallow the phantom taste that
teases your tongue,
before you finally rest your eyes on your stomach's
craving.
The first bite turns on your taste buds,
as you feel a striking pain in your jaw- your mouth
contracting with joy.
A jolt of flavour runs to your toes and back.
As the built-up anticipation carries the first few bites
down,
your eyes often bigger than your stomach.
The sharp pop of tangy cherry tomatoes,

the decadent, stringy cheese, clinging to your lip with a
buttery embrace,
the earthy mushrooms, and
the aery bread.
A cloud of steam rises as you dig in,
carrying the aroma and a warm hug for your nose
A burst of flavours,
of tamarind, salt, butter, rosemary, pepper and sautéed
garlic.
The utter joy of biting through a perfectly crusty,
browned breadcrumb batter,
your teeth gliding into the flavour packed, succulent
centre.
A velvety side of peppercorn sauce and
Roasted greens with a sprinkle of acidic vinegar.
Crunching the edible pearls on a pastry before devouring
the chocolate or
the over-baked flaky sides of a croissant before reaching
the luscious filling.
A feast for the senses,
A party in your mouth.
Every bite is a reward,
A fulfilment of desire.

14. Kintsugi

A fracture, a rupture, a relentless pull.
Fissures like lightning bolts, scar the ceramic vase.
Into pieces many,
only the shadow of its former self, left behind.
Life's burdens, like cannonballs, strike the stone wall of
the soul.
Dark lines emerge from the epicenter,
Chasms appear, marking the surface.
We stand like walls, occasionally attacked by flying
missiles with their target locked in.
Each scar, a testament, each crack, a story.
Off- balance, you scramble to gather the remnants again.
There may be beauty in the stripes that don us.
Time and again- picking up the pieces.
With cement and paint you patch up the wall to look
brand new.
Now, the cracks hidden and forced to be forgotten.
A jigsaw, pieces scattered, can be put back together,
a ceramic vase can be reconstructed with channels of
gold.
The chasms now filled with glistening acceptance.
Each fracture, a vein of hope-
scars that serve to stand out.
The shining yellow, a reminder that cavities can be filled

in.

The shadows in the crevasses shaped like bolts without
light,
now has a gold river flowing through,
illuminating the chasm once shattered,
it now shines.

15. The Sea

A rhythmic ascent. A crescendo.
Each drop of this liquid salt climbs up years' worth of
broken rocks.
The drops dissipate, into a blissful silence, heaven on
Earth, earthlings in heaven.

While your toes cling onto the handles of sand as the
floor shifts under your feet,
The water, bubbling with anticipation,
lures your body with crystal crumbs,
into the gurgling blue depths of another world.
The conductor raises their arms,
The baton- a wand of wind,
their arms violently vibrating from their waist till they
stand on their toes,
signalling the orchestra to swell like the highest wave.
The water crashes, fizzing out,
the orchestra now returning to the start of the musical
piece- only to play eternally.

Approaching a visit to the expansive unknown,
your senses pull a string,
a memory of experienced tranquillity.
Of a time where your feet tread the damp golden floor,

leaving imprints, both on Earth and in your mind.
Washed away by the indefatigable waves,
the crashing water erases the Earth's memory of the
footprint that once lay there,
for us to imprint on the earth's canvas once more.

Salt lingers in the air,
as the warm wind greets you with a tap on the tip of
your nose.
We bid our goodbyes as we retreat like the waves.
Footprints on gold, memories in mind,
washed by waves, erased with time.
You now long for this glistening infinity again.

16. Pain

A throbbing headache,
digging deeper into the nerves in your temples,
with each drum.
A cold nose,
the bridge tightening more as you breath the frigid air.
A sensitive tooth,
a pain that strikes the gum like lightning and
permeates through the jaw,
while your body takes a screenshot.
A shivering overworked muscle when you sit down the
wrong way or
an invisible laceration that electrifies the nerve when it
mingles with water.
A stubbed toe,
when you walk into the corner of your bed,
firecrackers, and loose sparks in you arm when your
elbow takes a hit.
Treating an open wound feels like rubbing sandpaper
over the exposed skin.
Physical and seen, this pain- apparent.

Emotional and buried, not often transparent.
Clinging on to indescribable feelings,
digging your nails into what is left of the fabric of

stability.

Attempting to grip onto a slipping rock.

Loosing, breaking- drops of affect run down your face.

Nipped heartstrings and clipped wings of hope.

Internal abrasions, often caused by unsolicited invasions.

An open wound in a covered chasm.

Pain is tangible and felt strongly when intangible.

A storm brewing inside that needs an escape.

A painkiller is a loved one, trusted, and understanding.

You swallow their advice as the pill clings to the slides of
your dry throat.

They provide you with a catalyst to ease the pain;

A hand that caresses wounds it cannot touch,

An embrace that wraps its hands around pain it cannot
feel.

17. Choose Now

Thrust into space; floating, bobbing with no land to
stand.
Cling onto a star they said-
one is strong but too small,
one is large enough but not sturdy,
and another wobbles, but can carry your body.
Choose, now!

As you float aimlessly;
being jostled around by space rocks and debris.
Should I dig my nails into the closest one?
Or should I calculate the odds for the best
while my mind continues to be the fulcrum for my
spinning body.
As my body spins, my mind cannot keep still,
I hesitate to hang on to one.
I must choose one, which one?
But I must choose, now!

I whoosh by the first; hands outstretched,
as my legs are sucked towards the second.
My body is moving faster than my mind can keep up,
my time running out, while I run out of breath.
I had not prepared for this day;

I procrastinated the task of choosing.
But the day is here,
I have missed one star,
two stars remain.

I must cling on to one; before I drift off, too far to swim
back.
Quick leaps of faith and I hang on to the star that will be
my fulcrum
till the time I can walk on land again.
I grasped, and am hanging in tight;
grateful to have three stars to choose from, in my sight.
I think it has always been- choose, now!
But I have grown to believe that I should choose NOW.

18. Wander

Eyes fixated on the blue ceiling, the ground crunching
under your feet.
Twigs caressing your arms and no end in sight.
The golden grains diving in between your toes
as the waves bring the ocean's saline embrace.
Clinging onto moss-greened rocks with the tips of your
fingers and toes,
the current of the cool water flowing against your feet.
The trees above have a hidden choir, singing in voices.
Jumping over puddle-dotted roads,
the smell of fried fish lingering in the air from the house
in the alleyway.

From a forest of trees to a jungle of concrete,
minuscule among glass giants,
your head on a turn table- left and right-
peering into shops of trinkets and stalls with omelettes.
Plastics of blue holding rainwater,
you walk at a snail's pace- your ears, overwhelmed with
the overlapping sounds;
your nose confused by the avalanche of smells.
A trance, interrupted by the prolonged horn of an
enraged driver.
Aimlessly walking in the air-conditioned igloo,

your eyes moving the hangers in every store.
Unaware of the time of the day,
unaware that you have been walking for hours on end.

A curated maze,
coloured rectangles on the walls and trees of metal at
every intersection.
Meandering through the works of another hand,
perusing the details.
A place of knowledge and colour, of art and splendour.

Bobbing on the dance floor,
your heart beating to the thump of the bass.
An obstacle track- pushing aside a hand, jumping over a
leg, avoiding a hair flip.
With a giant spinning wheel with seats and twinkles in
sight,
you walk against the current of the incoming crowd.

Tapping boxes that lead to circles and other boxes.
A black screen now blue,
words running away with the touch of a finger.

During the day, the body saunters through colours and
crowds.
As you close your eyes,
your mind meanders through worlds behind your eyes

and wanders,
as you stare,
now with your eyes closed,
at a blue ceiling.

19. Mosaic

More colours than the rainbow, closely set,
bound by a common mortar- being alive.
Broken and irregular, coming together to make up the
pixels of the world.
The Earth in space,
with its milky whites, cerulean blues,
forest greens, and wood browns.
A canvas of colour splashes;
a mosaic of tiny living things that make up a geoid.

Orange bleeding into blue sky,
the sun- an artist blending the colours on a canvas.
The grey-spotted moon,
lingers a bit longer before the blinding white flashes
above the horizon.

More colours that can be made on a palette, a
kaleidoscope of the living world.

The sapphire beaches that plunge into indigo.
The blue turning to black,
the surface that sees light, the bottom that lies in the
shadows.
The iridescent wings of the monarch butterfly,

reflecting light that makes the eyes see arctic and cobalt
blue.
Layering feathers of magnificent lapis;
The peacock gleans as the rain glazes its regal attire.

The breast of a feathered chirper- scarlet red staining its
white neck scarf.
The crimson petals that float on restaurant table centre
pieces,
the tomato red spaghetti surrounding the dotted
crimson.
The city is dotted with signal - red metal vessels,
transporting multi-coloured vials.
From the chilli red to the glistening rubies.

The deep orange stripes that mark the predators to
the marmalade - coloured clown-fish.
The pumpkins at fall and the sky before it turns to black.
Peaches and apricots, honey, and fire.

Wordsworth's crowd of golden daffodils,
the corncobs roasting on the beach,
the soft butter at breakfast,
the juicy pineapple,
and the filter on your eyes at dusk that renders the sky
mustard when rain is expected,
as the white sky changes to Prussian blue.

The sage green nodes of succulents,
the lemon green coat of a parrot,
the deep green after tossing basil in a wok and
the pitted olives that dot a pizza.
The leaves of trees, the colours of emeralds.
The signs of bravery that mark the uniforms of those
defending the country.

Purple auroras and pink bubble gum.
The colours of the world come together to blend into the
sphere that we dwell on.
A jigsaw puzzle of shades and tones,
of varied saturation and brightness.
A mosaic of different shapes,
a collage of countless colours.

20. Reflections

Still as glass,
until the raindrops create concentric circles.
A projection of the sky on the ground,
now dotted with grey.

A flash of something familiar
as you walk past the store-window.

The image of your likeness in the black glass,
before it lights up blue,

a fish eye distortion of your hands in the bathroom
faucet.

Upside down in the spoon as you eat;
both of you make a playing card;
your meal the king and queen of your hearts.

Thinking it is only you beholding yourself,
while the window rolls down.

Sweating and gasping for air in a hot kitchen,
you look up into the exhaust to view your perspiring
body.

You gaze at the fish waltzing in the pond
as you focus on your foreground,
you are now staring at the bobbing image of your
peering torso,
on the surface of the water.

As people sport black filters when the sun lets down an
avalanche of light,
you are talking to yourself,
as you stare at a moving mouth;
reading lips.

Examining the eyes of a loved one,
a faint wisp of your contours appears hazily on their
glazed iris;
seeing yourself how they might see you.

Deeply engrossed,
your expressions, a response to the happenings on
screen.
Ejected from the imaginary into the real world
as you stare at your disposition in the canvas of a device
that has gone to sleep.

Glass towers are decorated with the outlines of taller
glass towers in front of them.

The brightness of two suns at dusk;
from the sky and the window of a house facing west.

Those before us saw themselves in still waters,
marbled walls, and the glasses of their grandmothers-
transient, ephemeral.
Now a perfect, framed glass on the wall is
permanent evidence of our existence,
a clarity that may be destructive.
A mirror on the wall- a vision often designed,
a fleeting reflection- a truth unrefined.

21. After Today

Standing face to face with a frosted glass,
figures behind move,
but you cannot see any contours.
A mist of hope,
grey dancing shapes;
smoke from the fire of desire.
In the night, behind your eyes,
the shapes appear;
when it searches for clarity,
the morning comes.
After today, tomorrow will come,
a place within us, a place still unknown.
Pebbles in life's waters,
ripples reaching tomorrow.
A dormant volcano,
waiting for you to toss a burning match.
You sketch with pencils and erasers,
drafts upon drafts of detailed drawings on the wallpaper
of your eyelids.
As the curtains rise, the sketches now rolled up,
a blank canvas lays in front of you-
pick your favourite sketch to fill in with colour.
A working project, never complete.
Tomorrow will turn into today,

today into yesterday.
Calendars of tomorrows becoming todays.
Tomorrow is today unseen; tomorrow exists,
yet is waiting to be true.
Your mind is often chasing after tomorrow
when it could be running after today.